International Orality Network

ION Prayer Mobilization

An invisible, yet tangible platform of prayer...
I will lead the blind by ways they have not known, along unfamiliar paths I will guide them; I will turn the darkness into light before them and make the rough places smooth. These are the things I will do; I will not forsake them.
- Isaiah 42:16 (NIV)

This book is dedicated to Oral and Bibleless People Groups who still wait to hear the Gospel presented and given in a way they can really understand.

We are asking God to close the gap on LOSTNESS --the peoples of the globe that do not yet have the Good News or God's Word to guide them.

Table of Contents

We Invite You To Link in Prayer, Asking God for the Harvest

Let's Pray

Let's encourage others to pray and be diligent to ask for God to show us the Harvest!

orality.net/prayer/connecting-to-ion-prayer/

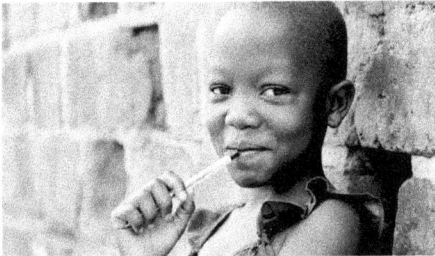

EVERY GREAT MOVE OF GOD

Started with a movement of prayer

We can all do our part in the work of the completion of the Great Commission:

Let's PRAY for the completion of Scriptures in the heart language of every people group.

For over ten years ION Prayer Teams have been praying together each Thursday. To help stay connected we offer a monthly prayer focus guide.

We invite you to pray with us!

orality.net/prayer/prayer-focus-updates/

Why Pray?

UUPG - Orality - Prayer - Bibleless

A little history of the International Orality Network (ION) Prayer. . .
A small group started out praying for Avery Willis, the first Executive Director, as he began the foundational work of the International Orality Network. Avery introduced them to the world of seeing the LOST, and praying through the work that was and is still needed to reach oral communicators. From that small group, God has launched a global prayer network serving ION.

This group realized the more they learned, the more they knew they did not know. The reality of the need remains the same. There are few numbers of believers who have an awareness of LOSTNESS or the Harvest as God sees these two as a priority in His work. It is our hope that this book and its content will help you to pray more effective and informed prayers. We encourage you to pray God centered and Spirit led prayers to Him as a priority.

Praying for the Orality Network

We invite you to pray each week with the International Orality Network (ION) as we see God continue to grow ION and bring forth new emerging regions. We invite you to visit the website and pray through the different areas. Thank you for linking and connecting in prayer.

How is ION Organized?:
https://orality.net/about/how-is-ion-organized/
Regions & Gateways:
https://orality.net/about/how-is-ion-organized/regions-gateways/

Did You Know?

- There are 4,000+ different languages currently spoken around the globe?
- Across the globe of those languages there are less than 700 full (OT/NT) Bibles Available?
- Of the FULL Bibles available, 178 are in the English language?
- There are 1,671 language groups that DO NOT have ONE VERSE of Scripture in their mother tongue and heart language?
- There are 1,002 languages with NO WRITTEN Scripture (book Bibles as in the letters to paper type that most of us use in the West)?
- There are 1,653 oral cultures whose languages have NO ORAL Scriptures (audio or digitalized)?
- Some resources are available in portions of Scripture or Scripture type resources, but 469 language groups still have NO Scripture Resources available at all (Gospel recordings, songs, oral Bible stories, Story sets or Scripture films)?

(Current Stats 2018)

We ask you to join in prayer — Father, Close the Gap!

We ask for a TURNAROUND in those who do not have one verse, to have FULL Bibles. Into the future may there be ZERO People Groups who will be in need of Scripture in their own heart language. Let us sing the song of Moses from Revelation 15:3-4 (RSV), *Great and marvelous are Your deeds, Lord God Almighty. Just and true are Your ways, King of the ages. Who will not fear You, O Lord, and bring glory to Your name? For You alone are holy. All nations will come and worship before You, for Your righteous acts have been revealed.* In Jesus name, amen.

International Orality Network and ION Prayer

ION seeks to radically influence the body of Christ to share Jesus with oral communicators in every people group.

ION is an affiliation of agencies and organizations working together with the common goal of making God's Word available to oral communicators in appropirate ways that enable church planting movements everywhere.

We invite you to get to know the International Orality Network. You can link with ION Prayer by visiting the Orality Network website: **orality.net**

Focusing Prayer on the Unfinished Task

10/40 Window:
- Least Reached
- Unreached (UPG)
- Unegaged Unreached(UUPG)
- Persecuted Church
- Oral Peoples
- Bibleless
- Largest populations of Children

What is a UPG?
Global Frontier Missions

10/40 WINDOW

TA ETHNE
AND THEN THE END WOULD COME   GOSP

2:59

Watch at
https://youtu.be/4nbXRuStiiE

Prayer Is Not A Formality, It Is The Foundation

"Prayer is not a formality, but a responsibility."
Dr. David Swarr
Executive Director, ION

The foundation of ION is an invisible, yet tangible platform of prayer.

"ORALITY refers to reliance upon the spoken, rather than written, word for communication. Orality is an ancient phenomenon that continues to the present... Purely oral societies pass along everything that matters from one generation to another without putting anything into writing. They rely on the spoken word including its sung and chanted forms." - International Orality Network

God Centered and Spirit Led

Seeing prayer being centered around God and His Kingdom, is not about our needs or what we think. Think about what Jesus said and did, as He modeled in John 5:19-24. God's plan is for the whole world to hear of His Son.

Much of what is done in the name of prayer is directed toward being man centered and need based. God continues to call us to come up higher, to join Him, even in the area of prayer. Remembering the challenge of John 16:33 (NIV), *In this world you will have trouble, but take heart for I have overcome the world.*

Everyone can pray

As the ION Prayer Team, we encourage our partners to link together in this key prayer point.

The point of the spear for ION is:
* Unengaged Unreached People Groups (UUPG)
* Oral and Oral Bibleless
* All Oral and Oral Preference Learners

We join in praying for:
#PRAY for ZERO
Zero Peoples without Scripture

How do we pray for Oral and Oral Bibleless?

We must include praying for Scripture for every people group in their mother tongue or heart language. Far too many have little to no access to the Scriptures or who are in fact Bibleless Peoples.

How Do We Share The Need to Pray?

* Partnerships, a wider team effort alongside each other
* Collaboration, a need for every part of the body of Christ to fit and step into the work
* Engaging the Global Church and Prayer Leaders, making space
* Encouragement for Global, National, Regional and Local Areas

For more information visit:
https://orality.net/prayer/about/

Overview

Praying Using this Book

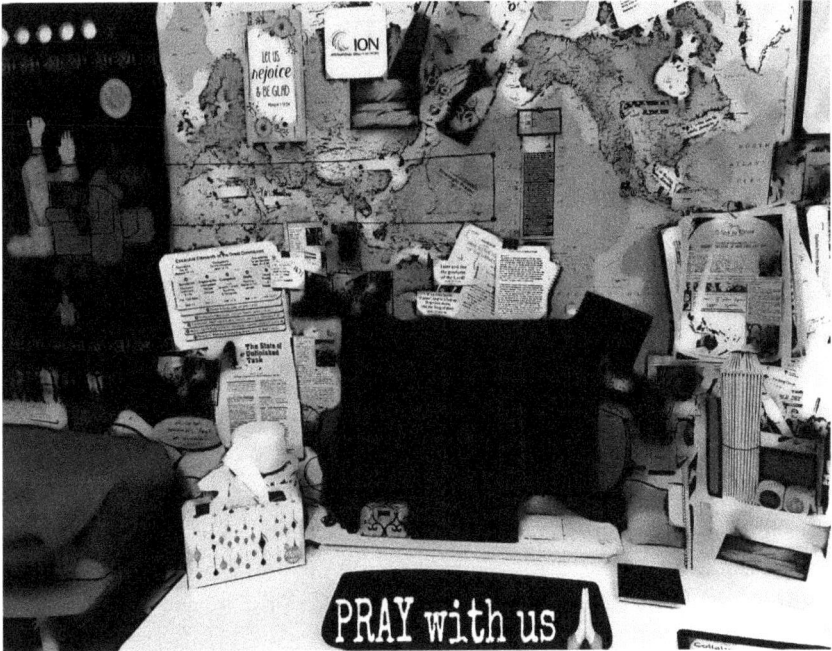

The purpose of this book is to help others to pray for Oral and Oral Bibleless People Groups, alongside of those working in the field of orality. ION Prayer publishes a monthly Prayer Focus guide to help everyone pray in a more united way. It is our hope that more people will embrace the need to change the way we present the Gospel to oral communicators, so all peoples can truly hear God's message and respond to the saving knowledge of Jesus Christ in a way they can really understand.

Prayer is essential to the work of God. It is His work.

Prayer is how we come into agreement with God.

Remembering prayer is best seen as a two way conversation between God and you. For far too long we have made prayer something "we do". Biblical patterns in Scripture for prayer support an active and intimate relationship with God. The recorded prayers seen in the Bible demonstrate and show prayer also being done in silence, in listening and in waiting with God.

Sharpen up your "listening skills" so that you can hear from the Father and then you can be more effective. As you pray through the prayers in this book, think differently about "what and how" you are praying.

God centered and Spirit led times of prayer may be new to you. Give yourself space to unlearn old patterns and allow the Holy Spirit to change habits of prayer where necessary. Give a portion of extra margin to allow for what the Spirit might be saying or in how He might want you to pray in this season of your life in Christ.

We thank you for being willing to pray for the Oral and Bibleless People Groups and their needs. We pray this book opens a whole new world of God's activity to you. As you learn more about Orality, you will be better equipped to pray in the model of effective informed intercession. This book was put together as a model of praying God's Word.

Praying Scripture might be new to you, it is one of the most practical ways to pray. Many of the books of the Bible contain prayers you can pray each day such as Paul's prayer in Ephesians 6:10-20.

For more on intentional listening please visit the website:
https://orality.net/content/intentional-listening-prayer/

Praying for UUPGs and Bibleless Oral Peoples...

Think about this...

How many Bibles do you have in your possession?
*   Currently there are 1,671 languages who do not have ONE VERSE OF SCRIPTURE in their heart language
*   How can that be? Here in the West we have the ENTIRE BIBLE, All 66 BOOKS available to all of us even in many different versions
*   Anytime we choose to, we are able to open our Bibles and take in God's Word into our hearts. Sadly that is not the case around the globe for millions of souls

Pursuing God for Spiritual Awakening and Global Harvest

We are looking for others who can see the reality of the need!
Asking God for the "more" of Ephesians 3:20-21.

To bring a transformation to the hearts and minds of those who pray for an understanding of current LOSTNESS and the BIBLELESS around the globe.

International Orality Network originated as an initiative of Table 71 which is a loose association of Christian organizations committed to working together in partnership among the remaining unreached people groups in the world. Table 71's goal is to see the number of people groups not reached get to zero and establish a strong and viable church within each of the UPGs.

Learn more about the history watch the video at **http://table71.org**

God's Mercy

Intro and Scripture

For God did not send the Son into the world to judge the world, but that the world should be saved through him. -John 3:17 (NIV)

This is good and acceptable in the sight of God our Savior, who desires all men to be saved and to come to the knowledge of the truth. -1 Timothy 2:3-4 (NASB)

The Lord is not slow about His promise, as some count slowness, but is patient toward you, not wishing for any to perish but for all to come to repentance. -2 Peter 3:9 (NASB)

So it is not [the] will of your Father who is in heaven that one of these little ones perish. -Matthew 18:14 (NASB)

The thief comes only to steal, and kill, and destroy; I came that they might have life, and might have [it] abundantly. -John 10:10 (NASB)

Prayer

I thank You Jesus, for the mercy that I have received. I declare that mercy triumphs over judgment, and I ask for Your mercy over Oral & Oral Bibleless People Groups. You did not come to condemn but You came to save. I ask You to send forth Your Holy Spirit to awaken Oral and Oral Bibleless People Groups to You. Bring them back as lost sheep into the fold. I thank You Jesus that Your mercy triumphs over judgment. In Jesus name, amen.

ION
INTERNATIONAL ORALITY NETWORK

Kathleen Dillard
ENCOUNTER GOD. IGNITE YOUR DESTINY.

Establish Gospel Friendly Gatekeepers

Intro

Everyone on the planet has the right to hear the truth of God's love for them, but in every people group there are gatekeepers that can restrict or allow the Gospel through to the people.

Scripture

It is He who changes the times and the epochs; He removes kings and establishes kings; He gives wisdom to wise men, And knowledge to men of understanding. -Daniel 2:21 (NASB)

Prayer

God, I thank You that we can look forward to the day when every knee will bow and and every tongue will confess that You alone are God. Help me Lord to do all I can to hasten that day and the return of Christ.

Lord, I know that in every place you have people who are friendly to the Gospel. I pray for the Oral and Oral Bibleless Peoples, and I ask Lord that You would raise up leaders and position gate keepers that would allow their people free access to Your truth. Put in place Lord, those who would open the door for Your servants, and serve the people by ushering in the truth of Your salvation. In Jesus name, amen.

Kathleen Dillard
ENCOUNTER GOD. IGNITE YOUR DESTINY

ION
INTERNATIONAL ORALITY NETWORK

Bible Translations

Intro
Having the Bible translated into the local language is an important resource for reaching an unreached people group. The written Word in their own language adds validity and acceptance to the message.

Scripture
For the word of God is living and active. Sharper than any double-edged sword, it penetrates even to dividing soul and spirit, joints and marrow; it judges the thoughts and attitudes of the heart. -Hebrews 4: 12 (NIV)

Prayer
Lord Jesus, You are the God of all, the faithful God who keeps covenant and mercy for a thousand generations with those who love You and keep Your commandments. Lord I want to see the Oral and Oral Bibleless People Groups be some of those who love You and keep Your commandments.

Father I thank You for Your Word, and for those who sacrificed so much over the years so that I could have the Bible in my language. What a blessing it is to read Your truth anytime I want. I pray Lord that You would provide that same blessing to the Oral and Oral Bibleless People Groups.

I ask that You would accelerate the translation and distribution process for all languages. I bless those who are working on this in Jesus name. I ask that You would release Your favor and grace upon them, and abundantly provide the funds they need to get Your Word out to the Oral and Oral Bibleless People Groups. In Jesus name, amen.

ION
INTERNATIONAL ORALITY NETWORK

Kathleen Dillard
ENCOUNTER GOD. IGNITE YOUR DESTINY

Invite Them to the Lord's Banquet

Intro

Jesus died for every tongue, tribe and nation. As His ambassador, you have the privilege of inviting them to the Lord's banquet.

Scripture

And the LORD of hosts will prepare a lavish banquet for all peoples on this mountain; A banquet of aged wine, choice pieces with marrow, And refined, aged wine. -Isaiah 25:6 (NASB)

Prayer

I thank You Lord for preparing a banquet for us, and for giving us free access through Your sacrifice. You are the Lord high and lifted up, and You reign forever and ever and there is no end to Your Kingdom.

As a servant of the Most High God, I announce the coming of the Lord's banquet, and I speak to the Oral and Oral Bibleless People Goups now in Jesus name. Your place Is reserved at the Lord's table. Your seat has been purchased by the blood of the Lamb. We need them there, to complete the worship of our Savior on that day.

I speak across the heavens In Jesus name and I invite the Oral and Oral Bibleless People Groups to join us at the Lord's table. I proclaim in the heavenlies that they are welcome and are needed to complete the body of Christ. Jesus has prepared the way for them in His love and His grace. In Jesus name, amen.

Kathleen Dillard
ENCOUNTER GOD. IGNITE YOUR DESTINY

ION
INTERNATIONAL ORALITY NETWORK

Exalt God above their gods

Intro and Scripture

For you, LORD, are the Most High over all the earth; you are exalted far above all gods. -Psalm 97:9 (NIV)

Prayer

Lord, I lift Your name up over Oral & Oral Bibleless People Groups and worship You as the one and only true and living God. You are their creator, You know their past, present and future, You are the only One worthy of their worship. I exalt Your name above every spirit, and every so-called god that Oral & Oral Bibleless People Groups look to for help.

I proclaim Your sovereignty and authority over these false gods. Lord, You are the God of heaven, and You are highly exalted above all other gods. There is no one who can challenge the authority of Your love.

Jesus, You alone died for Oral & Oral Bibleless People Groups' salvation and I raise the banner of Your love over them right now, and proclaim that they have been purchased by Your sacrifice. Let the worship of Your name break through the deception that holds Oral & Oral Bibleless People Groups back from knowing You, and may the angels soon rejoice. In Jesus name, amen.

ION
INTERNATIONAL ORALITY NETWORK

Kathleen Dillard
ENCOUNTER GOD. IGNITE YOUR DESTINY.

Thrust out Workers

Intro
There are people groups who still have no one to tell them about Jesus. Millions of people would respond to Christ, if they only knew. We need people who are willing and equipped to go.

Scripture
He told them, "The harvest is plentiful, but the workers are few. Ask the Lord of the harvest, therefore, to send out workers into his harvest field." -Luke 10:2 (NIV)

Prayer
Lord, I thank You for pursuing me when I didn't know You. I thank You for putting people in my life and bringing people across my path that were willing to introduce me to the lover of my soul.

I know it is not Your will that any should perish, so I lift up the Oral and Oral Bibleless Peoples to You now. I ask You Lord of the harvest to send forth workers into the harvest field of the Oral and Oral Bibleless Peoples.

Stir the hearts of Your people Lord. Call to them as they pray, as they sleep, as they worship. Agitate them, and shake them free from whatever holds them back. Lord, I ask that You would commission a fresh workforce to pursue the Oral and Oral Bibleless Peoples with Your love, that Your name might be glorified in their midst. In Jesus name, amen.

Men and Women of Peace - Protection

Intro
When there is no witness for the Gospel in a town, village, or tribe, the people need a 'person of peace'. Someone whose heart is soft toward the Gospel, who will receive the servants of the Lord and not turn them away. These people are key and we should bless them with God's protection.

Scripture
The LORD will protect him and keep him alive, And he shall be called blessed upon the earth; And do not give him over to the desires of his enemies. -Psalm 41:2 (NASB)

Prayer
Lord, You are a shield, a strong tower. You are a fortress and our hiding place. You are the God over all the earth, and there is no one who can challenge Your power.

I pray for the men and women of peace among the Oral and Oral Bibleless Peoples and I ask that You would protect them from the attacks of the enemy. Cause Your angels Lord to encamp around them and keep them from the evil one.

Lord, I ask that You would protect their life and not surrender them to the desire of their foes. For the sake of the Gospel among the Oral and Oral Bibleless Peoples, I ask that You would cover these friends of truth with Your wings, and overshadow them with Your mighty presence. In Jesus name and for His sake, amen.

Victory for the Harvest

Intro
Ministry is really a battle between light and darkness. Let's stand with our spiritual soldiers, as Moses stood watching Joshua in battle (Exodus 17:10-13), and pray in faith the promises of God until the victory comes.

Scripture
Bless all his skills, LORD, and be pleased with the work of his hands. Strike down those who rise against him, his foes till they rise no more.
-Deuteronomy 33:11 (NIV)

Prayer
Lord, I acknowledge that the battles Your servants face belong to You. You are mighty God. Send Your angels to war in the heavenlies on behalf of those working among the Oral and Oral Bibleless Peoples today.

Defeat the liar and the thief. Smite the loins of those who rise up against these workers according to Your Word. Push back the darkness by Your power and release victory over this harvest. Raise up Your holy standard for all to see.

Let the King of glory come in among the Oral and Oral Bibleless Peoples. Give Your servants eyes to see the victory at hand and all the warriors fighting beside them. Fill them with faith and boldness to fight on for Your glory. In the mighty name of Jesus, amen.

Kathleen Dillard
ENCOUNTER GOD, IGNITE YOUR DESTINY

ION
INTERNATIONAL ORALITY NETWORK

Angelic Visits

Intro
All through human history God has used His angels as messengers, even announcing the birth of Christ to the shepherds. God loves to use His people, but there are times when only an angelic visit will do the job.

Scripture
And the angel answered and said to him, "I am Gabriel, who stands In the presence of God; and I have been sent to speak to you, and to bring you this good news." -Luke 1:19 (NASB)

Prayer
God of mercy and grace, thank You for Your heart to seek and save those that are lost. You are the Good Shepherd who leaves the ninety-nine and goes out after the one.

I agree with Your desire that none should perish, and I lift up the Oral and Oral Bibleless Peoples before Your wonderful throne of grace. For those who have no access to Your truth Lord, I'm asking You to dispatch Your angelic messengers.

Visit key people among these groups, and bring them the revelation of who Jesus is. Just as You announced the birth of Christ to the shepherds, I ask for an announcement to be sent to the Oral and Oral Bibleless Peoples.

Extend Your mercy Lord, command Your servants, and send them on their way. Reveal Christ to those who have no revelation, and rescue them as the Good Shepherd that You are. In Jesus name, amen.

ION
INTERNATIONAL ORALITY NETWORK

Kathleen Dillard
ENCOUNTER GOD. IGNITE YOUR DESTINY

Strategy for Workers

Intro

Gaining access and favor among an unreached people group can be very tricky. Workers need the wisdom of God to navigate cultural, political and religious issues.

Scripture

But the wisdom that comes from heaven is first of all pure; then peace-loving, considerate, submissive, full of mercy and good fruit, impartial and sincere. -James 3:17 (NIV)

Prayers

Lord, You are the beginning and the end, the Alpha and Omega, and there is nothing hidden from Your sight. You are the wisest counselor of all. I thank You for Your promise, that You give wisdom to those who ask.

I'm asking now for Your servants working with the Oral and Oral Bibleless People Groups, that You would give them the strategies they need today. Fill them with heavenly wisdom that is pure, peace-loving, and considerate. Reveal to them the divine strategies they need to navigate the cultural issues they are facing with the Oral and Oral Bibleless People Groups.

Inspire them with creative solutions to the political and religious challenges that hold back the Gospel among the Oral and Oral Bibleless People Groups. Lord, release Your wisdom and light the path before them to penetrate these people groups with the truth of Your love. In Jesus name, amen.

Kathleen Dillard
ENCOUNTER GOD. IGNITE YOUR DESTINY.

ION
INTERNATIONAL ORALITY NETWORK

Revelation for a Father

Intro
In every people group there are fathers who love and provide for their children. They each have something in them that connects with our Father in Heaven. Our prayers can focus the attention of the Holy Spirit on one of these fathers.

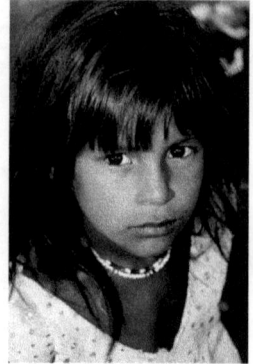

Scripture
Who would not fear You, O King of the nations? Indeed it is Your due! For among all the wise men of the nations. And in all their kingdoms, there is none like You. -Jeremiah 10:7 (NASB)

Prayer
God of Glory, who can be compared to You? You are faithful and true, redeeming that which Is lost and restoring that which is broken. You are worthy of all our worship and devotion.

Lord, You are the greatest father of all, and I know that Your heart aches over Your children who do not yet know You. I pray for the Oral and Oral Bibleless People Groups today and I agree with Your heart for them. I join with You Lord in Your longing to touch them, and I focus my prayer today on one of the fathers. The one who is crying out for peace. Lord, You know who he is, and I'm agreeing with Your heart for him. Visit him Lord with Your presence, and comfort him with Your revelation. Break in upon the darkness of his soul with Your wonderful light.

Draw this father into fellowship with You Lord, and begin a legacy In his family that will honor You for generations to come. In Jesus name, amen.

ION
INTERNATIONAL ORALITY NETWORK

Kathleen Dillard
ENCOUNTER GOD. IGNITE YOUR DESTINY.

Stir Bibleless People Groups to Hunger for God

Intro

Sometimes people get used to living in spiritual poverty, because they don't know anything else. However, the Lord has put a deep need for Him in the heart of every man, woman and child. In prayer, we can ask the Lord to stir up this yearning, and prepare the way for His powerful message of reconciliation and restored relationship.

Scripture

For even if there are so-called gods whether in heaven or on earth, as indeed there are many gods and many lords, yet for us there is but one God, the Father, from whom are all things, and we exist for Him; and one Lord, Jesus Christ, by whom are all things, and we exist through Him. -1 Corinthians 8:5-6 (NASB)

Prayer

Lord, I thank You that You are the God of truth, and that Your word says, "You shall know the truth and the truth shall set you free.". Thank You for the freedom that You bring in every area of our lives. Right now I ask You to release a yearning and a restlessness within Oral and Oral Bibleless People Groups, a real spiritual hunger that won't settle for a substitute.

Lord, stir them with such a strong desire, that they would embrace any change or venture any risk necessary, in order to encounter Your Truth. I thank You Lord for hearing my prayer, and for the hunger You are stirring in Oral and Oral Bibleless People Groups. In the mighty name of Jesus, amen.

Kathleen Dillard
ENCOUNTER GOD. IGNITE YOUR DESTINY

ION
INTERNATIONAL ORALITY NETWORK

Spiritual Leaders Come to Christ

Intro

Leaders are gatekeepers in the community and are key to opening doors for the Gospel. When they have a revelation, they tell everyone about it. If they have an encounter with Christ, everyone will hear about Him.

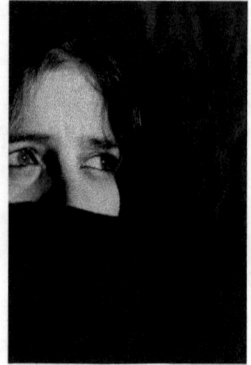

Scripture

The LORD has made His salvation known and revealed His righteousness to the nations. -Psalm 98:2 (NIV)

Prayer

Lord, You are the true God, and there is no other. Your name is above all other names. There is no one who is like You, no one who can compete with Your love and faithfulness. Your name is worthy to be shouted from rooftops and glorified in every place on earth!

Lord, make Your Name known to the Oral and Oral Bibleless People Groups. Let today be the day of salvation for one of the spiritual leaders of the Oral and Oral Bibleless People Groups.

I ask for dreams and visions and powerful encounters with Your Spirit, that would offer undeniable evidence that You alone are God. Let him shout the news of Your Son from all the high places, and open a gateway to the Oral and Oral Bibleless People Groups for the Good News.

Break down the deception that clouds his mind from Your truth, and release the revelation needed to embrace Christ as his Savior. Cause his life to be a powerful testimony of Your truth and redemption. In Jesus name, amen.

ION
INTERNATIONAL ORALITY NETWORK

Kathleen Dillard
ENCOUNTER GOD. IGNITE YOUR DESTINY.

Dreams That Reveal Jesus

Intro

Dreams are accepted in many cultures as a source of revelation. God has often revealed Himself through dreams and visions. This is especially important among Unreached Peoples where there is little or no witness.

Scripture

And it will come about after this; that I will pour out My Spirit on all mankind; And Your sons and daughters will prophesy, Your old men will dream dreams, Your young men will see visions. -Joel 2:28 (NASB)

Prayer

Lord, You have the name that is above all names. You are Lord forever and there is no one who can challenge Your authority and power. You rule forever and ever, and there is no end to Your Kingdom.

Lord, you have promised in Your Word that You would pour out Your Spirit in the last days. So, I am asking for an outpouring of revelation for the Oral and the Oral Bibleless People Groups. They are made in Your image, and You know them each by name, but they don't know You, the lover of their soul.

I'm asking God that You would reveal yourself tonight through dreams and visitations. Visit the leaders of households, and villages, and the spiritual leaders with Your truth. Speak to the Oral and Oral Bibleless People Groups in a way they can understand, and reveal to them that Jesus is the One they are looking for, the Prince of Peace.

Kathleen Dillard
ENCOUNTER GOD, IGNITE YOUR DESTINY

ION
INTERNATIONAL ORALITY NETWORK

Silence the Accusations

Intro and Scripture

He who vindicates me is near. Who then will bring charges against me? Let us face each other! Who is my accuser? Let him confront me! It is the Sovereign LORD who helps me. Who is he who will condemn me? -Isaiah 50:8-9a (NIV)

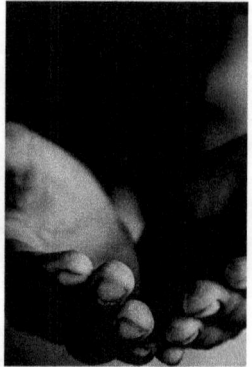

Prayer

Lord, there is no God like You in heaven above or on earth beneath. You are the One who keeps covenant and shows loving-kindness to Your servants who walk before You with all their heart.

I thank You Lord for being the One who vindicates Oral and Oral Bibleless People Groups. I thank You Jesus for being their advocate, and for standing with them to confront their adversary.

I stand with Jesus now, before the judge of all the earth, and reject the accusations Satan would make against Oral and Oral Bibleless People Groups. It is the sovereign Lord who helps them, redeems them, and sets them free. No accusation or condemnation can stand before the cross of Christ.

Thank You Jesus for Your sacrifice, and redemption, and for being the advocate that stands between Oral and Oral Bibleless People Groups and their accuser. In Jesus name, amen.

ION
INTERNATIONAL ORALITY NETWORK

Kathleen Dillard
ENCOUNTER GOD. IGNITE YOUR DESTINY

Protect and Preserve

Intro and Scripture

The LORD will protect him and keep him alive, And he shall be called blessed upon the earth, And do not give him over to the desire of his enemies. -Psalm 41:2 (NASB)

Prayer

Lord, You are the One who rides the ancient skies above, who thunders with a mighty voice. Nothing is hidden from Your sight, and nothing is beyond Your reach. What You bless is blessed and what You protect is protected.

Lord, I come before Your mighty throne of grace to pray for Oral and Oral Bibleless People Groups. Your Word says that You are the One who protects and preserves. So I look to You Lord, and I ask for Your protection now over Oral and Oral Bibleless People Groups.

As they go out today to serve others, I ask that You would be a shield about them, that You would bless them in the land, be their rear guard, and not surrender them to their foes. Honor Your Word Lord and make them yet another testimony for Yourself today. In Jesus name, amen.

Joy

Intro and Scripture
Shouts of joy and victory resound in the tents of the righteous: "The Lord's right hand has done mighty things!" -Psalm 118:15 (NIV)

Prayer
Lord, You are the One who makes rivers to flow on barren heights, and springs within the valleys. You turn the desert into pools of water, and the parched ground into springs. You bring joy out of despair, and nothing is beyond Your reach.

I exalt Your name Lord over Oral and Oral Bibleless People Groups, I declare that You are high and lifted up over the circumstances of their lives. You are their hope and their joy; their salvation and their God. The One who chose them from the foundation of the world. The One who paid the price for their redemption.

Lord, You are the One who loves them with an everlasting love, who leads them and guides them with Your eye upon them. Release to them Lord a fresh flow of joy and celebration for who You are and what You have done for them. In Jesus name, amen.

ION
INTERNATIONAL ORALITY NETWORK

Kathleen Dillard
ENCOUNTER GOD. IGNITE YOUR DESTINY.

Jesus My Teacher

Intro and Scripture

You call Me Teacher and Lord; and you are right, for [so] I am. -John 13:13 (NASB)

With Him are wisdom and might; To Him belong counsel and understanding. -Job 12:13 (NASB)

I will instruct you and teach you in the way which you should go; I will counsel you with My eye upon you. -Psalm 32:8 (NASB)

Take My yoke upon you, and learn from Me, for I am gentle and humble in heart; and you shall find rest for your souls. -Matthew 11:29 (NASB)

Good and upright is the Lord; Therefore, He instructs sinners in the way. -Psalm 25:8 (NASB)

Prayer

Jesus, I thank You for being the teacher of the Oral and Oral Bibleless People Groups. Though You know all things in heaven and on earth, still You bid them to come. I'm so grateful that they can find a place at Your feet. Lord, help them to lay down the cares of this world and take up Your yoke.

Teach them how to enter into Your rest. Let them wait upon You, until their strength has been renewed like the eagle.

Jesus, teach them more about childlike faith and simple trust, resting when they need to rest in You, and persevering in prayer when they just need to go the second mile. Speak to them Lord. Thank You Jesus for being the Teacher. In Jesus name, amen.

Kathleen Dillard
ENCOUNTER GOD. IGNITE YOUR DESTINY

ION
INTERNATIONAL ORALITY NETWORK

Hope

Intro and Scripture

Why, my soul, are you downcast? Why so disturbed within me? Put your hope in God, for I will yet praise him, my Savior and my God.
-Psalm 42:11 (NIV)

Prayer

Lord of all Hope, You answer us with awesome deeds of righteousness, O God our Savior, the hope of all the ends of the earth and of the farthest seas, to whom shall we look?

Lord, we live in a fallen state and our souls struggle against the world, the flesh and the devil. Despair can sometimes catch our heel, and we lose sight of the hope we have in You.

I come before You today, and I ask You to guard the hope of the Oral and Oral Bibleless People Groups. Deliver them, Lord from discouragement and fear that can creep in and wear them down. Break in upon their minds today Lord and dislodge doubts, and troubling thoughts.

Give them fresh strength to praise and exalt Your name in the midst of difficulty, and birth yet another testimony of Your deliverance into their lives. In Jesus name, amen.

ION
INTERNATIONAL ORALITY NETWORK

Kathleen Dillard
ENCOUNTER GOD. IGNITE YOUR DESTINY.

Renewing the Mind

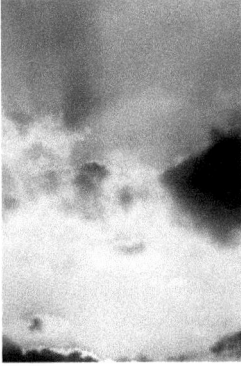

Intro and Scripture

Do not conform to the pattern of this world, but be transformed by the renewing of your mind. Then you will be able to test and approve what God's will is his good, pleasing and perfect will.
-Romans 12:2 (NIV)

Prayer

Lord, high and lifted up, You rule from a kingdom far above our understanding. You are the Alpha and Omega, the One who knows all things, and there is no end to Your Kingdom.

I pray for Oral and Oral Bibleless People Groups today, as ones who have been redeemed from darkness into Your glorious kingdom of light, and I ask Holy Spirit that You would renew their minds today. Transform them Lord, by releasing a deeper understanding of who You are. Break down the barriers of their natural thinking and birth in them divine revelation that honors and glorifies You.

As Oral and Oral Bibleless People Groups seek to love You with all their heart, mind, soul and strength, give them the understanding they need to walk in Your ways. Complete the work You have begun in them Lord, and display their lives as a billboard of who You are. In Jesus name, amen.

Kathleen Dillard
ENCOUNTER GOD, IGNITE YOUR DESTINY

ION
INTERNATIONAL ORALITY NETWORK

Escapes From Death

Intro and Scripture

God is to us a God of deliverances;
And to GOD the Lord belong escapes from death.
-Psalm 68:20 (NASB)

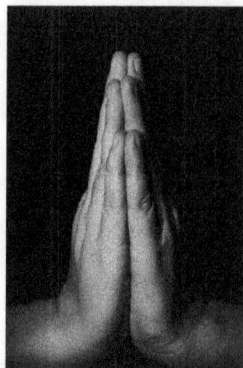

Prayer

Lord, all power belongs to You. You rule and reign, unchallenged in the heavens. You are far above all rule and authority, power and domin- ion, and every title that can be given, bring Your espcapes from death to the Oral and Oral Bible- less People Groups, today.

I receive Your word Lord, "*to GOD the Lord belong escapes from death*". I ask that You would deliver from danger and from the jaws of death, those who have been caught up in crisis. You are the God of the impos- sible, and I ask that You would release impossible escapes for these innocent men and women today.

Stand in the midst of the afflicted Lord, and call them out from the shadow of death. Extend Your hand of deliverance Lord, and honor Your name with a miracle today. In Jesus name, amen.

No Anxiety

Intro and Scripture
When anxiety was great within me,
your consolation brought joy to my soul.
-Psalm 94:19 (NIV)

Prayer
Lord, there is no one else like You. You form the light and create darkness. You bring prosperity and create disaster. You are the sovereign God who does all these things.

Lord, I bring Oral and Oral Bibleless People Groups before You and I ask that You would guard their hearts from anxiety and fear. I recognize that fear is the devil's tool, and position Your faithfulness, Your truth, and Your mighty promises between the devil's fearful lies and Oral and Oral Bibleless People Groups' hearts today.

Stir in Oral and Oral Bibleless People Groups' hearts Lord, that unexplainable faith and confidence that comes only from You. Guard their minds from fearful thoughts and that inward dialog that drags us down the road to despair. Break the power of the evil one over their minds today, shatter his lies, and bless Oral and Oral Bibleless People Groups with joy that refreshes the heart. In Jesus name, amen.

Kathleen Dillard
ENCOUNTER GOD. IGNITE YOUR DESTINY.

ION
INTERNATIONAL ORALITY NETWORK

Bless Their Household

Intro and Scripture

Now be pleased to bless the house of your servant, that it may continue forever in your sight; for you, Sovereign LORD, have spoken, and with your blessing the house of your servant will be blessed forever. -2 Samuel 7:29 (NIV)

Prayer

Who among the gods is like You, O LORD? Who is like You - majestic in holiness, awesome in glory, working wonders? You alone are worthy of all our praise.

Lord, You are the God who loves to bless, so I bring Oral and Oral Bibleless People Groups before You now and ask for a mighty blessing on their household this week. Extend Your scepter Lord, and decree a blessing for them.

May their hearts be overwhelmed by Your blessing and mercy. May they be surprised by Your goodness and humbled by Your generosity. May they testify to the truth that You do all things well, and more than we could ever hope or imagine. Bless them Lord with a testimony that honors Your name. Amen.

Direct Their Steps

Intro and Scripture

For I command you today to love the LORD your God, to walk in obedience to him, and to keep his commands, decrees and laws; then you will live and increase, and the LORD your God will bless you in the land you are entering to possess. -Deuteronomy 30:16 (NIV)

Prayer

Lord, You are the God of all knowledge, the One who knows the end from the beginning, You are the Alpha and Omega.

Lord of promise, I thank You for Your instructions on how we should live. I present Oral and Oral Bibleless People Groups before You Lord, and I ask that You would direct their steps today to walk in Your ways, so that You can bless them in the place where they serve.

At each turn and each decision today Holy Spirit, I ask that You would speak, and give them ears to hear, that they may keep Your commands and do what is pleasing in Your sight.

Shout Your warnings Lord, keep them on the straight path, and pluck their feet out of the net, keep them from evil Lord, so that You may bless them. I pray in Jesus name and for His glory, amen.

Kathleen Dillard
ENCOUNTER GOD. IGNITE YOUR DESTINY

ION
INTERNATIONAL ORALITY NETWORK

Wisdom

Intro and Scripture

If any of you lacks wisdom, you should ask God, who gives generously to all without finding fault, and it will be given to him. -James 1: 5 (NIV)

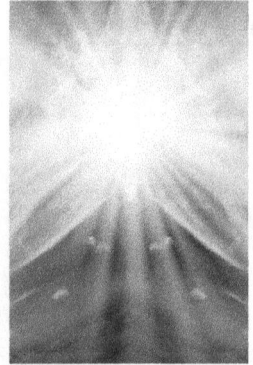

Prayer

Lord, You created the heavens with a word and fashioned the earth with Your voice. You have more wisdom in one thought than in the entire universe.

Lord, I thank You for Your promise to give wisdom to us when we need it. With the challenges that Oral and Oral Bibleless People Groups face today, they need wisdom. Lord, I present them before Your great throne and ask for Your wisdom to be poured out to them now. Give them a generous portion according to Your Word. Divine wisdom which is pure, peace loving, full of mercy and good fruit.

Fill Oral and Oral Bibleless People Groups Lord with wisdom that will honor You. Give them solutions that will bless the good, confound the wicked, strengthen the weak, and break the yoke of injustice. Clear the channels Lord, between Oral and Oral Bibleless People Groups and Your throne, and let Your wisdom flow like a river. In Jesus name, amen.

Bless the Skill of the Leaders

Intro and Scripture
Bless all his skills, LORD, and be pleased with the work of his hands. -Deuteronomy 33:11a (NIV)

Prayer
Lord, you are the author of all the skills of man. You are the God of all the earth, and of the highest heavens. Your gaze takes in the universe, and yet You know each one of our thoughts.

I bring the leaders of Oral and Oral Bibleless People Groups before You right now, and ask that You would be pleased with the work of their hands. Bless their skills Lord, and undergird them as they seek to lead Oral and Oral Bibleless People Groups. For the sake of the people, Lord, I ask You would reveal divine solutions to them today Lord, and cause them to act decisively in the face of today's challenges.

Anoint these leaders in the work You have called them to, and give them wisdom to overcome every obstacle. Honor the hope Lord, of the people of Oral and Oral Bibleless People Groups who trust in these leaders to serve their best interest. In Jesus name, amen.

Kathleen Dillard
ENCOUNTER GOD. IGNITE YOUR DESTINY

ION
INTERNATIONAL ORALITY NETWORK

Trouble – Open Doors for the Gospel

Intro

When epidemics or natural disasters strike, or trouble that just comes to individuals and families, the results can be devastating. Often, in the midst of this difficulty and uncertainty there comes an opening for the Gospel.

Scripture

LORD, my strength and my fortress, my refuge in time of distress, to you the nations will come from the ends of the earth and say, "Our ancestors possessed nothing but false gods, worthless idols that did them no good. -Jeremiah 16:19 (NIV)

Prayer

Lord, You are the good shepherd. You look after each one of Your children. You are the only safe refuge and fortress in times of trouble.

Lord, today some of the Oral and Oral Bibleless People Groups are facing trouble they cannot manage. They are in need of Your help. I ask Lord, that You would respond to their need, and come to their aid.

Use this crisis to introduce them to Your goodness. Allow this difficulty to soften their hearts to Your truth. Give them the grace they need to walk away from the god who has failed them and embrace You as their only Lord and Savior. Open their eyes Lord to see You as the lover of their soul, their refuge, and their fortress. In Jesus name, amen.

Meet Bibleless in the Lonely Places

Intro and Scripture
But Jesus often withdrew to lonely places and prayed. -Luke 5:16 (NIV)

Prayer
Lord, You are the Father of compassion and the God of all comfort, who comforts us in all our troubles. You are the One who never chan-ges, and You know all the concerns of our hearts.

Lord, I call Your attention to Oral and Oral Bibleless People Groups right now. Would You please visit with them today Lord? Jesus, You often went to lonely places to pray, I'm asking that You would go to that lonely place within Oral and Oral Bibleless People Groups today and pray with them.

Prince of Peace, give them a glimpse of what peace with You is like. Touch them in their loneliness and be the comfort that they need.

Reveal Yourself to them as One who understands, and be the companion that comforts them. Lord, show Yourself to Oral and Oral Bibleless People Groups as the God of all comfort, and break down the barriers that hold them back from Your love. In Jesus name, amen.

Kathleen Dillard
ENCOUNTER GOD. IGNITE YOUR DESTINY.

ION
INTERNATIONAL ORALITY NETWORK

Bless Their Good Deeds

Intro and Scripture

Blessings crown the head of the righteous.
-Proverbs 10:6a (NIV)

What the righteous desire will be granted.
-Proverbs 10:24b (NIV)

The prospect of the righteous is joy.
-Proverbs 10:28a (NIV)

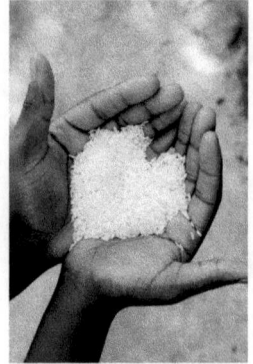

Prayer

Lord, You are a righteous and generous God, You hear the cries of the weak and reward the deeds of the just. You shower all Your creation with blessings and pour down on all Your creatures the gift of life. From Your hand comes every good thing, and from You all blessings flow.

I bring Oral and Oral Bibleless People Groups before You Lord and remind You of Your nature to bless. Please look down on Oral and Oral Bibleless People Groups with Your favor and reward them for every good deed and every desire to do good. Grant to them, Lord the desires of their hearts, and make them a channel of Your blessings. Let Your blessings pour down upon their head, and fill their hearts with hope. In Jesus name, amen.

Culturally Sensitive TV and Radio

Intro

Reaching the unreached is a monumental task. There just aren't enough individuals to get the word out to everyone. TV and radio can be incredibly powerful mediums for communicating the gospel, because they can penetrate areas where Christian workers may not be able to go.

Scripture

It has always been my ambition to preach the gospel where Christ was not known, so that I would not be building on someone else's foundation. -Romans 15:20 (NIV)

Prayer

Lord, I thank You for all the unique cultures and languages You have created. You know and understand all of them. Thank You that even in places we cannot go, You are there.

Lord, I ask that You would anoint and appoint workers to create relevant, culturally sensitive Christ-centered radio and TV for the Oral and Oral Bibleless People Groups. Aid them as they research the culture, and give them divine insight and inspiration in their presentation of the Gospel.

I ask that You would bless them with brilliantly creative ideas to communicate Your truth, and that the Oral and Oral Bibleless People Groups would be receptive to Your message. I ask Father that You would give the workers favor with people in the media business, and that You would bless them with all the resources, provision, and volunteers they need. Anoint these media presentations to break through the darkness and shine the light of Your truth. In Jesus name, amen.

Kathleen Dillard
ENCOUNTER GOD. IGNITE YOUR DESTINY

ION
INTERNATIONAL ORALITY NETWORK

Individuals: Revelation for a Leader

Intro
In every people group there are leaders who guide the activities of others. They each have something in them that connects with the God of the universe. Our prayers can focus the attention of the Holy Spirit on one of these leaders today.

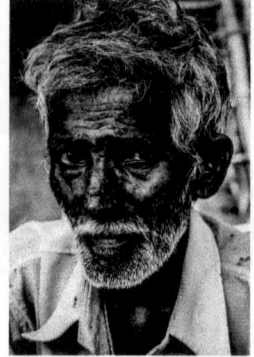

Scripture
The LORD reigns, let the nations tremble; he sits enthroned between the cherubim, let the earth shake. -Psalm 99:1 (NIV)

Prayer
God of creation, Your Glory exceeds our understanding. You manage the universe in ways we cannot imagine. Your ways are perfect, and Your love is everlasting.

Lord, I lift up the Oral and Oral Bibleless People Groups to You, and I pray for the leaders among them, the ones who have honor and respect among the people. I single out one of these leaders today Lord, and agree with You for his heart to be opened. Bind the demonic spirits that challenge Your authority and hold back the revelation of Your love.

Pour out extra grace to him today, Lord. Pull back the curtains of deception, and flood his heart with revelation of who You are. Overshadow him with Your presence Lord, and touch him with the truth of Your love. Draw him near to You Lord, give him eyes to see beyond what he knows. Comfort him with Your peace and reveal to him the Jesus who died for his freedom. In Jesus name, amen.

ION
INTERNATIONAL ORALITY NETWORK

Kathleen Dillard
ENCOUNTER GOD. IGNITE YOUR DESTINY.

Miracles Confirming the Word

Intro
Words have little meaning, especially in places where physical needs are great. It takes the miraculous to capture the hearts of the people. In places where embracing Christianity means abuse and persecution, believers need to be sure they have accepted the true God.

Scripture
So Paul and Barnabas spent considerable time there, speaking boldly for the Lord, who confirmed the message of His grace by enabling them to perform signs and wonders. -Acts 14:3 (NIV)

Prayer
Lord, I pray for the Oral and Oral Bibleless People Groups and I ask for miracles to confirm the truth of the Gospel, that deceptions would be shattered, believers would be strengthened in their faith, and unbelievers would be challenged to let go of false beliefs.

Lord, release Your power to those who are at work among the Oral and Oral Bibleless People Groups, that the truth of Your word would be confirmed. Enable Your servants Lord, to perform miracles and wonders that break the power of superstition and deception.

As my prayer goes up to You Lord, let Your power come down, and reveal the truth of who You really are to the Oral and Oral Bibleless People Groups. In Jesus name, amen.

Kathleen Dillard
ENCOUNTER GOD. IGNITE YOUR DESTINY

ION
INTERNATIONAL ORALITY NETWORK

Reveal the Man of Peace

Intro
When there is no witness for the Gospel in a town, village, or tribe, you need a 'man of peace'. Someone whose heart is soft toward the Gospel, who will receive the servants of the Lord and not turn them away.

Scripture
Go; behold, I send You out as lambs in the midst of wolves. Carry no money, no bag, no shoes; and greet no one on the way. Whatever house you enter, first say, 'Peace be to this house.' If a man of peace is there, your peace will rest upon him; but if not, it will return to you. -Luke 10:3-6 (NASB)

Prayer
Lord Jesus, You are worthy of all glory and honor and praise. There is no other God besides You, and one day every knee will bow and every tongue will confess that You alone are Lord.

Lord of the Harvest, I come before you now for the sake of the Oral and Oral Bibleless People Groups, and I ask for the men and women of peace to be revealed. As your servants move forward to bring the truth of Your love, I ask that You would send to them these men and women of peace.

Arrange divine appointments that would bring Your servants into contact with them. Put an expectation in their hearts that will cause them to receive Your servants with favor. Establish them as an anchor point for the Gospel among the Oral and Oral Bibleless People Groups. In Jesus name, and for Your glory, amen.

ION
INTERNATIONAL ORALITY NETWORK

Kathleen Dillard
ENCOUNTER GOD. IGNITE YOUR DESTINY

Culture Keys for the Gospel

Intro

With every culture God has preserved for Himself a testimony. Pray that these culture keys would be revealed and spark a hunger in the people to know more.

Scripture

"For from the rising of the sun even to its setting. My name will be great among the nations, In every place incense is going to be offered to My name, and a grain offering that is pure; for My name will be great among the nations," says the LORD of hosts. -Malachi 1:11 (NASB)

Prayer

Lord, You are the true and living God, You rule over all things visible and invisible. The nations belong to You, and You have woven into the fabric of every culture a testimony to Your name.

I bring the Oral and Oral Bibleless People Groups before You now. I ask Lord, that You would reveal those things in their culture, that reflect who You are and Your Son Jesus. Cause the hidden treasures of Your truth to be brought up and displayed for all to see.

Lord, use these keys of insight to ignite a curiosity and hunger among the Oral and Oral Bibleless People Groups to know more about who You are. Give Your servants wisdom and strategy to use these keys to promote the Gospel among these people groups. In Jesus name, amen.

Kathleen Dillard
ENCOUNTER GOD. IGNITE YOUR DESTINY.

ION
INTERNATIONAL ORALITY NETWORK

Worship God Over Oral and Oral Bibleless Peoples

Intro and Scripture

Who is this King of glory? The LORD strong and mighty, the LORD mighty in battle. Lift up your heads, you gates; lift them up, you ancient doors, that the King of glory may come in. Who is He, this King of glory? The LORD Almighty - he is the King of glory. -Psalm 24:8-10 (NIV)

Prayer

O God, Your praise reaches to the ends of the earth; Your right hand is filled with righteousness.
You are the everlasting God, the Creator of the ends of the earth. The earth is Yours and all it contains: every nation, tribe, family, and city.

Lord, I acknowledge that there are spiritual forces at work against Oral and Oral Bibleless People Groups. There are gods in the land that oppress and manipulate them, but You are the King of Glory, and I worship You as the God of all the earth.

You alone are worthy to rule over their lives because You gave Your Son for them. No other god, no spirit, no spiritual power or forces of darkness can resist Your claim to Oral and Oral Bibleless People Groups because You alone have paid the price.

I worship You Lord as God of all the earth, God of all creation, God of Glory, God of redemption, and God of Oral and Oral Bibleless People Groups. May You be exalted today over their lives. In Jesus name, amen.

ION
INTERNATIONAL ORALITY NETWORK

Kathleen Dillard
ENCOUNTER GOD. IGNITE YOUR DESTINY

Government Leaders Opposing the Gospel

Intro
Everyone on the planet has the right to hear the truth of God's love for them, but many times, Government leaders restrict their people from having access to the Gospel. Through prayer we can see this change.

Scripture
It is He who changes the times and the epochs; He removes kings and establishes kings; He gives wisdom to wise men, and knowledge to men of understanding. -Daniel 2:21 (NASB)

Prayer
God, I thank You that we can look forward to the day when every knee will bow and every tongue will confess that You alone are God. Help me Lord to do all I can to hasten that day and the return of Christ.

I lift up the Oral and Oral Bibleless People Groups to You Lord, and I ask that You would move on their behalf. You are one who puts leaders in place and who removes them. I ask Lord that You would test the hearts of those leaders among the Oral and Oral Bibleless People Groups, and remove from their position those who would oppose the Gospel. Give them no place of influence or authority over the people. Sweep them aside, and do not allow them to hinder the work of Your servants any longer. In Jesus name, amen.

Kathleen Dillard
ENCOUNTER GOD. IGNITE YOUR DESTINY.

ION
INTERNATIONAL ORALITY NETWORK

Revelation for a Pioneer

Intro
In every people group there are pioneers who are ready to break with their culture and tradition, and explore something new. Our prayers can focus the attention of the Holy Spirit on one of these pioneers.

Scripture
Declare his glory among the nations, his marvelous deeds among all peoples. -1 Chronicles 16:24 (NIV)

Prayer
Lord, You are God over all the earth, Your kingdom extends beyond the heavens. There is no one more worthy of praise than You. You are God, and there is no one else.

Lord, I lift up the pioneers among the Oral and Oral Bibleless People Groups, those who have a drive to explore new places and new ideas. Who are not satisfied with what is, but are always longing for what could be.

Holy Spirit, I ask that today You would visit one of these pioneers and spark in their mind the revelation they need to embrace the Good News of Jesus. Fuel their heart for discovery to seek Your truth, and Your face.

Break them free from traditions and superstitions. Stir their pioneering spirit to search for the one true God, and carve a path for others to follow. In Jesus mighty name, amen.

ION
INTERNATIONAL ORALITY NETWORK

Kathleen Dillard
ENCOUNTER GOD. IGNITE YOUR DESTINY.

God's Favor for Workers

Intro

Workers cannot get the job done without the help of people outside of and within, the community they are trying to reach. They need support financially, logistically, and a solid network to help them further the cause of Christ in unreached regions.

Scripture

Their descendants will be known among the nations and their offspring among the peoples. All who see them will acknowledge that they are a people the LORD has blessed. -Isaiah 61:9 (NIV)

Prayer

Lord, You own everything. The earth is Yours, and everyone on it. You open doors that no man can shut. You are sovereign. If You are for us, no one can be against us.

God, I thank You for all the workers that are reaching out to the Oral and Oral Bibleless People Groups. Lord, let Your favor shine on them today, and open doors for them in the community. I ask for divine appointments and connections with influential people who can give them access to the opportunities and resources they need.

Lord, I ask that Your favor would give them access to people and places that are impossible to reach. Bless their finances and other resources with Your favor, that every need they have today would be met. Thank You Lord for blessing Your workers. Your Your Word says, "Let all who see them acknowledge that they are a people the Lord has blessed". May Your name be glorified among the Oral and Oral Bibleless People Groups! In Jesus name, amen.

Kathleen Dillard
ENCOUNTER GOD. IGNITE YOUR DESTINY

ION
INTERNATIONAL ORALITY NETWORK

Disappointed with their Religion

Intro

People need a good reason to stop believing one thing and start believing something else. Let's pray for dissatisfaction with their current beliefs. Ask God to reveal to them the shortcomings of their beliefs, so their hearts will be open for His truth.

Scripture

But where are your gods which you made for yourself? Let them arise, if they can save you in the time of your trouble; -Jeremiah 2:28a (NASB)

Prayer

Lord, there is no other God besides You, a righteous God and a Savior. There is none except You. You are the only God that never disappoints, You are always faithful, and always true.

I bring the Oral and Oral Bibleless People Groups before you now, and I ask Lord, that You would reveal the shortcomings of their gods. Challenge the impostors and show them to be silent idols. Lord, I ask for a demonstration so the Oral and Oral Bibleless People Groups could see the impotence of their gods.

Stir a deep disappointment in the hearts of the Oral and Oral Bibleless People Groups and cause them to question their devotion and worship. Wean them from their dependence on their gods, to make room in their hearts for You. In Jesus name, amen.

Let There Be Light

Intro and Scripture

The true light that gives light to everyone was coming into the world. He was in the world, and though the world was made through Him, the world did not recognize Him. He came to that which was His own, but His own did not receive Him. Yet to all who received Him, to those who believed in His name, He gave the right to become children of God. -John 1:9-12 (NIV)

Prayer

Lord, You are the Alpha and Omega, the beginning and the end, nothing is hidden from Your sight. You are the One who said, "Let there be light", and there was light.

Lord, say it again now to Oral and Oral Bibleless People Groups, that Your light might shine into their hearts. Let Your light fall upon them, and reveal the truth of who You are. Penetrate the darkness that conceals Your identity as the lover of their souls, and flash the light of Your revelation into their hearts.

Lord, You are the light of the world. Reveal something today that will bring them closer to You. Chase out the shadows that hide who You are and illuminate a portion of their darkness that will never be dark again. In Jesus name, amen.

Kathleen Dillard
ENCOUNTER GOD, IGNITE YOUR DESTINY

ION
INTERNATIONAL ORALITY NETWORK

Bind the Deception

Intro

Scripture is clear that our battle is not against flesh and blood but against spiritual forces of darkness. All unreached peoples have some kind of belief system. They have all accepted a counterfeit for the true and living God. We must bind this deception so they can be free to receive the truth.

Scripture

For all the gods of the nations are idols, but the LORD made the heavens. -Psalm 96:5 (NIV)

Prayer

Lord, how awesome are Your deeds! There is no one who is mighty like You. You are Lord over all the nations of the earth. You have made the heavens, the earth and everything on it, the seas and all that is in them.

Father, Your Word says that Jesus has been given all authority over heaven and earth. It also says that what I bind on earth is bound in the heavenlies. I stand right now in the authority of Jesus, and I bind the spirit of deception that has captured the minds of the Oral and Oral Bibleless People Groups. In Jesus name, amen.

ION
INTERNATIONAL ORALITY NETWORK

Kathleen Dillard
ENCOUNTER GOD. IGNITE YOUR DESTINY

Acknowledgement for the collaboration of prayer content used in this booklet

We want to give credit and a huge thank you for the collaboration and use of prayer content in this booklet:

**Thank you, Kathleen Dillard for permission,
www.kathleendillard.com**

On each of the prayer pages you will see
this acknowledgment to Kathleen:

Kathleen Dillard
ENCOUNTER GOD. IGNITE YOUR DESTINY.

www.kathleendillard.com

Lord, Close the Gap!

Need

There is little to no access to the Scriptures for far too many peoples of the world. We acknowledge the reality of. . . 7,102 languages in the world, yet only 664 have a full and complete Bible. – 4.2.20 Foundation

Prayer

Father, we pray for You to close the gap in the area of peoples (5.7 Billion) of the world of which 80% are oral, who have limited to no access to the saving knowledge of Jesus Christ through His Word in a way they can really understand!

Far too many have little to no access to the Scriptures or who are in fact Bibleless Peoples.

We link together in prayer for the completion of Scripture for all languages in our lifetime.

We are praying for the innovative ways You are bringing to make the reality of Revelation 5:9 and 7:9 possible. In Jesus name, amen.

We invite you to join to PRAY for Zero

#PrayforZero
    - Let there finally be zero people groups without God's Word

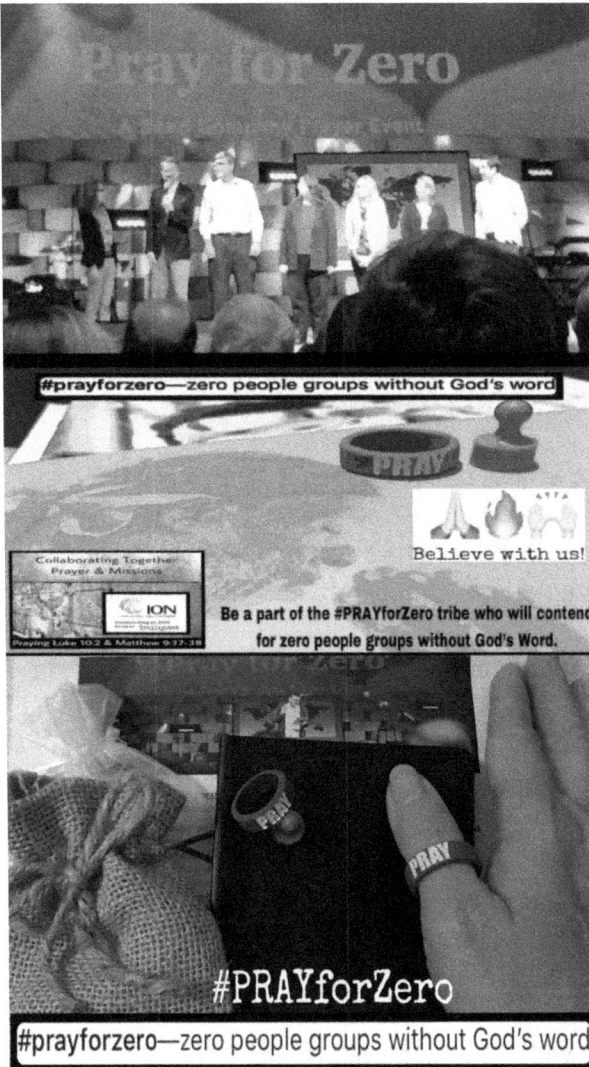

Definitions

Bibleless: People groups who do not have Scripture in their heart language or mother tongue. Scripture can be available in different categories: 1) Written Scripture; 2) Oral Scripture; 3) Portions & Stories; 4) Audio & Video.

Church Planting Movements: Fundamentally disciple-making movements. Discipleship here is defined as growing in Christlikeness over time. While discipleship begins immediately at conversion, and sometimes even before conversion, it continues for a lifetime. (Source: Church Planting Movements / David Garrison, **http://churchplant-ingmovements.com**)

Heart language or mother tongue: The language that a person learns from birth and speaks in their home while growing up that speaks to their heart in a way that brings transformation. (Source: International Orality Network, **http://orality.net**)

Little to no access to the Gospel of Jesus Christ: Places in the world where the Gospel is not — no believers, no missionaries, no outreach work, no church, no Scripture portions or Bibles available.
(Source: International Orality Network, **http://orality.ne**t)

Oral communicators: People from all over the globe, from all walks of life and all levels of education who communicate primarily through oral, not textual means. 80% of the world's population are oral communicators —approximately 5.7 billion people.

These include:
• 2.7 billion unreached people in approximately 3,500 unengaged, unreached people groups
• Approximately 2 billion people are without any of the Old Testament
• 1,800+ unengaged, unreached people groups consisting of 350 million people without a single verse of Scripture in their heart language

- 1.35 billion oral communications who may be literate, but prefer to learn and communicate through oral means
- Over 1/2 of this number is made up of children
(Source: International Orality Network, **http://orality.net**)

Person of Peace:
The person of peace is essentially a "point person". This person may be spiritually seeking, or already a believer. The person of peace is: 1) open to the message of Jesus 2) receptive to the messenger 3) influential in their social network, and bringing others to the message. These three factors converging in a single individual can be a catalytic hub for the Gospel. (Source: Act Beyond, **http://beyond.org**)

The 10/40 Window:
The 10/40 Window is home to the majority of "unevangelized" people who may have a minimal knowledge of the gospel but have no valid opportunity to respond to it. Nearly two-thirds of the world's people reside in the 10/40 Window. (Source: Joshua Project, **http://legacy.joshuaproject.net/10-40-window.php**)

Unengaged Unreached People Groups (UUPG): Have no known full-time workers on the ground involved in evangelism and church planting. Currently, the number is at 910 groups (last updated July 31, 2018). (Source: Finishing The Task, **http://FinishingtheTask.com**)

Unreached People Groups (UPG): It is estimated that of the 7.47 billion people alive in the world today, 3.15 billion of them live in unreached people groups with little or no access to the Gospel of Jesus Christ. According to Joshua Project, there are approximately 16,800 unique people groups in the world with about 6,900 of them considered unreached. The vast majority (95%) of these least reached groups exist in the 10/40 window and less than 10% of missionary work is done among these people. (Source: Joshua Project, **http://joshuaproject.net**)

Getting Started

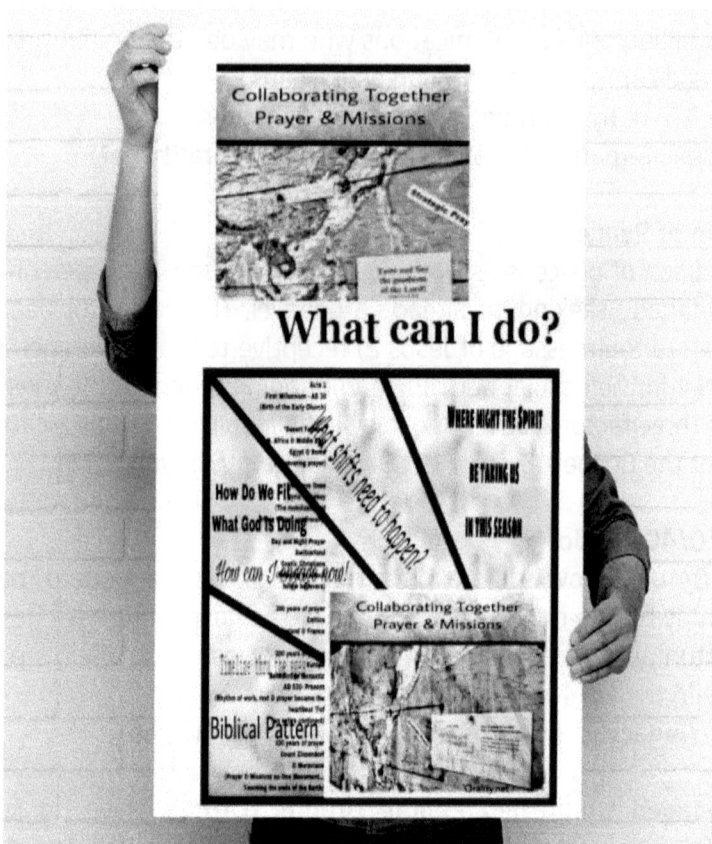

What Can I Do?

— Prayer As Strategy

— YOU can Pray!

Pray with us: Father, return us to the place where prayer is our priority.

See this article showing the history of prayer over the ages: **https://ionprayer.com/2017/04/12/pray-therefore-to-the-lord-of-the-harvest-that-he-may-send-out-laborers-into-his-harvest-luke-102/**

We invite you to join the Orality Movement of ION

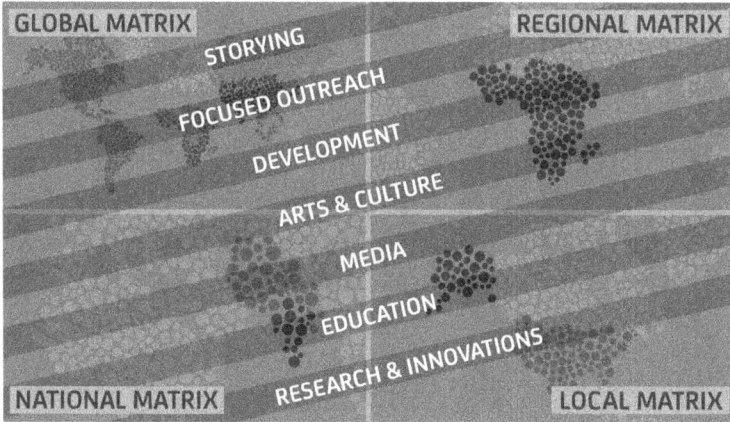

7 Gateways and Multiple Pathways for Service

Storytelling
Crafting; practice of; training

Focused Outreach
Church planting; youth & children; secondary orality; minorities & indigenous peoples; diasporas; students; women; family; refugees; victims of disaster

Development
Community; medical & health; crisis & relief; social action & justice; market place & business

Arts & Culture
Narrative; drama; poetry; music; visual

Media
Mass; Collective; Micro; audio/video scripture engagement; tools and methods; publishing

Education
(Formal; informal; non-formal education) Theological, pastoral, marketplace, government, affinities (women emerging, etc.)

Research & Innovation
Statisrics; metrics; projects methodologies

Bible in 90 Days Prayer Initiative

Bible in 90 Days - A different kind of prayer initiative

Praying and Washing in the Word daily, for the last three months of the year, ASKING in prayer for Scripture and Scripture Access to be available for the Every & All.

Asking the Lord, "Close the gap!" Let there be Scripture (FULL BIBLES) available for everyone. We Pray Luke 10:2 and Matthew 9:37-38, *Pray the Lord of the Harvest, Send the laborers into His harvest field*. In Jesus name, amen.

To learn more about this prayer initiative visit: **https://orality.net/ prayer/bible-in-90-days-prayer-initiative/**

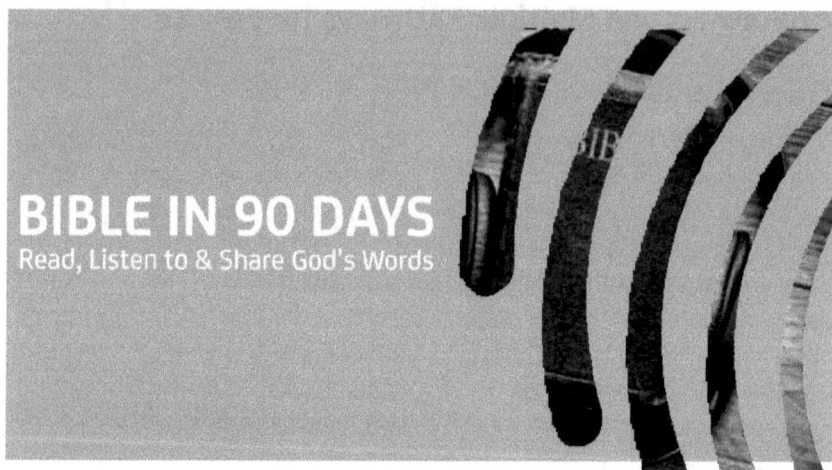

BIBLE IN 90 DAYS
Read, Listen to & Share God's Words

Orality Network partners take the last 90 days of the year in focused prayer, "LISTENING to God's Word in Audio and join in united prayer for the Bible to made available to everyone around the globe in their heart language and mother tongue".

Bring the ION Prayer Floor Map to your group!

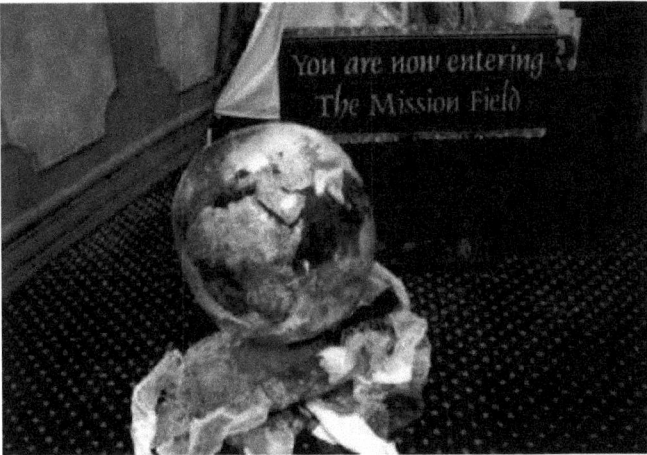

To request the ION Prayer Floor Map to come to you contact **IONPrayer@gmail.com**

ION
INTERNATIONAL ORALITY NETWORK

Every great move of God ...
... started with a movement of prayer.

Think about the story in 2 Chronicles 20 and the strategy of God .. "You will not need to fight in this battle. Position yourselves, stand still and see the salvation of the LORD." It was a significant step of faith for the people of Israel to position themselves, to stand still, and to believe God as they faced the battle in front of them (vs. 18-19). God allows His strategy to be seen, as they are led by singing worshipers (vs 20-21). This is quite a different model than most use today.

Are we willing to follow God In His plan of prayer? In this story, they prayed God centered, Kingdom focused, and Spirit led prayers, focused on the reality of what God can and will do. Prayer like this makes prayer times come alive. It allows the pray-ers to be up, alert and engaged, where everyone is working together, led by God. The correct response to God is worship and praise, not more laboring. This biblical model will accelerate the finishing of the Great Commission. In this story, their only cry was a song, "Praise the LORD, for His mercy endures forever". They did not rest on their own merits or strengths, but trusted God.

Read about the history of our ION Prayer Teams in Chapter 15 of the book titled, "Orality Breakouts" - **https://orality.net/library/other/orality-breakouts**

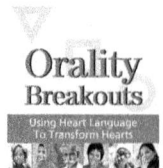

Orality Breakouts
Using Heart Language To Transform Hearts

ION seeks to link with others in prayer support mobilization to bring the body of Christ into the reality of what it might take to reach oral communicators, who are 80% of the world.

Visit us at:	www.orality.net
ION Prayer Blog:	IONPrayer.com
Twitter:	@IONPrayer
Email:	IONPrayer@gmail.com

orality.net

Praying for Oral and Oral Bible-less People Groups
Copyright © International Orality Network, 2018

ISBN: 978-1-7326983-1-4
First Published, August 2018

Published by International Orality Network
a network of The Lausanne Movement

www.orality.net
www.lausanne.org

PO BOX 23023
Richmond
VA, 23223
USA

info@orality.net
--

ION

INTERNATIONAL ORALITY NETWORK

Praying for:

Oral and Oral Bibleless
People Groups